Message to Parents/ Teachers

In order for this Bible study wordbook to be profitable for your children, your help is needed. Try to be available to answer questions that might arise, but please, as much as possible, allow your children to discover these important Bible truths for themselves.

Instructions for Parents/Teachers

1. This Bible study wordbook entitled *Giving* addresses the issues of giving to one's local church. A parent or another adult can work with the student to complete this study. The wordbook is part of a series that is most beneficial when used together. Other wordbooks in this series include *Salvation, Baptism, Communion* and *Church.*

2. Allow your student to study the material on his/her own as much as possible. Children in early elementary grades might need assistance in completing some sections of the wordbook.

3. You should grade the fill-in sections and the final quiz. Review the answers and be sure your student understands the issues involved. The quiz answers are on page 3.

4. At home set the money aside that children want to give at church before Sunday morning. Some families have containers in which each child can place his/her offering money. You can make a container or buy one. Families—especially those with younger children—might use a container in the shape of a church. This would reinforce the destination and purpose of the offering. Check with your local Christian bookstore for the availability of these banks. You can also look for woodcrafters that make banks in the image of a church.

5. Explain how to use offering envelopes at your church. Parents might consider filling out the envelope in the presence of their older elementary students. Discuss how you have decided how much to give and where to direct it.

6. Teachers should explain the various ways offering money is utilized for accomplishing God's work at the church. Consider inviting one of the church leaders to make a presentation to the class. A family could invite one of their church leaders to their home to discuss what happens to the money at the church once it is placed in the offering.

7. Tithing is presented in this wordbook as regular, planned giving to God's work through a student's local church. Avoid communicating anything that resembles the old "nickel in the plate" pattern where you scrounge for some loose change as the offering plate comes around. This teaches nothing about giving. Children learn about the New Testament concept of giving by giving from their own resources. Perhaps their resources involve an allowance or money earned from performing small jobs.

8. The directions you give your students should vary according to their age. You will probably need to encourage younger students to give a portion to the Lord's work at your church. The higher grade-level students should be given the freedom to make their own decisions about their giving.

9. Loving the Lord with all your heart is the concept used in this wordbook to point out that a person becomes a believer by joining God's family. This concept is presented as God's requirement before someone gives money to the Lord through his or her church. II Corinthians 8:1–7 is an extended passage that points this issue out. Review the student's answers on pages 6 and 19.

Quiz Answers (Pages 22–23):

True/False: **1.** F **2.** F **3.** T **4.** T **5.** F **6.** T **7.** Review it yourself **8.** Jesus Christ **9.** God's bank in heaven

Pastor Richard E. Todd is Senior Pastor of Community Grace Brethren Church in Whittier, California. He first joined the staff there in 1982 as Associate Pastor and became Senior Pastor in 1987. He and his wife, Claudia, have three sons: Ryan, Riley and Rory.

GIVING

WingSpread Publishers

Chicago, Illinois

www.moodypublishers.com

An imprint of Moody Publishers

Giving: A Bible Study Wordbook for Kids
by Richard E. Todd
ISBN: 978-1-60066-197-6
Printed by Versa Press in East Peoria, IL – 07/23

Printed in the United States of America

5 7 9 10 8 6 4

Cover illustrations by Rick Hemphill
Interior design by Pam Fogle

Originally published by Crosswalk Resources

1

Why Do People Give Money to Their Church?

WHY?

People give money to their church so that others will be able to hear how much God loves them.

The Apostle Paul thanked the Christians at the church in the city of Philippi for the money they had sent him. Paul told them that their gift helped him pay for food and other things so he could spend more time telling the people in the cities he traveled to about how much God loves them.

"You people in Philippi remember when I first preached the Good News there. When I left Macedonia, you were the only church that gave me help. Several times you sent me things I needed." Philippians 4:15–16

Write one way your church uses the money people give so that others will hear about God's love:

WHY? People give money to their church because God wants them to share what He has given to them.

"Our Lord and God! You are worthy to receive glory and honor and power. You made all things. Everything existed and was made because you wanted it."
Revelation 4:11

The Bible says in Genesis 1:1 that God created the heavens and the earth. Because God made everything, He owns it. God created the heavens and the earth . . . they belong to Him because He made them. God wants us to take care of what He has made.

Write one thing that God has made inside each arrow.

The Things That Are Mine Also Belong to God!

1. This belongs to me: ______ → This is how it **also** belongs to God: ______

2. This belongs to me: ______ → This is how it **also** belongs to God: ______

3. This belongs to me: ______ → This is how it **also** belongs to God: ______

4. This belongs to me: ______ → This is how it **also** belongs to God: ______

5. This belongs to me: ______ → This is how it **also** belongs to God: ______

6. This belongs to me: ______ → This is how it **also** belongs to God: ______

WHY? **PEOPLE GIVE MONEY TO THEIR CHURCH TO THANK GOD FOR ALL HE'S DONE FOR THEM.**

"You are rich in everything—in faith, in speaking, in knowledge, in truly wanting to help, and in the love you learned from us. And so we want you to be rich also in this gift of giving. You know the grace of our Lord Jesus Christ. You know that Christ was rich, but for you he became poor. Christ did this so that by his being poor you might become rich." 2 Corinthians 8:7, 9

Don't the people who love you give you gifts?

WHO ARE TWO PEOPLE WHO HAVE SHOWN THEIR LOVE FOR YOU BY GIVING YOU A GIFT? *Write their names in the tags below.*

JESUS GAVE HIS LIFE SO THAT WE COULD HAVE THE GIFT OF ETERNAL LIFE WITH HIM. JESUS GAVE EVERYTHING BECAUSE HE LOVES US.

WHY? People give money to their church knowing that God will reward them in heaven.

"Store your treasure in heaven. The treasures in heaven cannot be destroyed by moths or rust." Matthew 6:20

Below are some things that God says are important only on earth. *Place a check in the column that tells about the things that God says are important on earth and also in heaven.*

	Treasure on earth only	Treasure on earth and in heaven
1. Witnessing to your friend.	◯	◯
2. Giving money to help a missionary pay his bills.	◯	◯
3. Winning a baseball game.	◯	◯
4. Praying for a neighbor who is sick.	◯	◯
5. Collecting comic books.	◯	◯
6. Taking food to a shelter for homeless people.	◯	◯
7. Now you write one: ______________________	◯	◯

WHY?

People give money to their church because they have first given God what He really wants.

Finish this song that a child sang during a Christmas play:

"What shall I give Him, poor as I am. If I were a shepherd, I would give Him a lamb. If I were a wise man, I would do my part. So what shall I give Him? I'll give Him my ______ ."

Connect the dots from 1 to the number 13 to find a picture of the missing word.

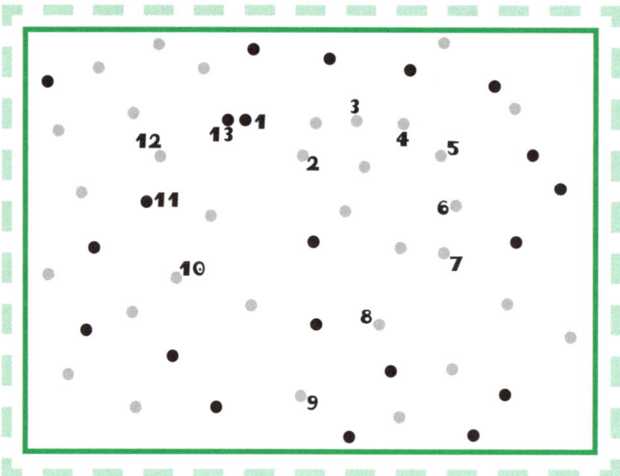

What does it mean for a person to give this to the Lord?

______

What Happens to the Money People Give?

WHAT?

The money people give at church is collected during a special time in the service.

The ushers collect the money people give at church. The money is then counted and put in the bank. But it doesn't stay at the bank.

Churches don't save money—they give it!

Read Acts 13:1–5. *Place a check in the circle that tells another way your church uses some of its offering money.*

Some of the money people give at their church helps:

- ◯ Pay the pastor and others who work at their church.
- ◯ Missionaries go and work in other parts of the world.
- ◯ Meet the needs of people in special ways.

Read 1 Timothy 5:17–18. *Place a check in the circle that tells another way your church uses some of its offering money.*

Some of the money people give at their church helps:

- ◯ Pay the pastor and others who work at their church.
- ◯ Missionaries go and work in other parts of the world.
- ◯ Meet the needs of people in special ways.

Read 1 Thessalonians 5:12–15. *Place a check in the circle that tells another way your church uses some of its offering money.*

Some of the money people give at their church helps:

- ◯ Pay the pastor and others who work at their church.
- ◯ Missionaries go and work in other parts of the world.
- ◯ Meet the needs of people in special ways.

WHAT?

SOME OF THE MONEY PEOPLE GIVE TO THEIR CHURCH HELPS PAY THE BILLS.

YES NO

DOES YOUR CHURCH RENT THE BUILDING IT MEETS IN? *If it does, then some of the offering helps pay the rent.*

DOES YOUR CHURCH HAVE LIGHTS THAT USE ELECTRICITY? *Some of the money people give to your church pays for the cost of electricity.*

DO YOU GET SPECIAL PAPERS AT CHURCH TO TAKE HOME THAT HAVE STORIES ABOUT PEOPLE WHO LOVE JESUS? *Offering money helps pay for these papers.*

DOES YOUR CHURCH HAVE A VAN, BUS OR CAR TO HELP PEOPLE TRAVEL TO CHURCH AND SPECIAL ACTIVITIES? *If so, then gasoline and car repairs are part of how the offerings are used.*

NOW IT'S YOUR TURN. WRITE SOMETHING THAT COSTS MONEY AT YOUR CHURCH.

Coin Pile

God wants us to give money to our church
to thank Him for all He's done for us.

How many coins are there below? ________

COLORING PAGE

3 How Much Money Should I Give to My Church?

HOW MUCH?

You should start giving to your church.

When you receive money from work or an allowance, you can start giving part of it to your church. People give because they are obeying what God has commanded in the Bible. You do not have to be a certain age to start giving at your church.

"On the first day of every week, each one of you should put aside as much money as you can from what you are blessed with." 1 Corinthians 16:2

YES	NO	
○	○	**Do you receive money for work you do?**
○	○	**Do you receive an allowance from your family?**
○	○	**Do your parents say it is OK to give part of the money you receive to your church?** *Your parents may give you money to put in the offering when you are younger. As you get older, you should decide how much of your money to give.*

HOW MUCH?

You should give to your church what you <u>want</u> to give.

The people in the churches in Macedonia "gave much because of their great joy. . . . No one told them to do it." 2 Corinthians 8:2–3

HOW MUCH?

You should give to your church what you <u>are able</u> to give.

"Jesus sat near the Temple money box where people put their gifts. He watched the people put in their money. Many rich people gave large sums of money. Then a poor widow came and gave two very small copper coins. These coins were not worth even a penny. Jesus called his followers to him. He said, 'I tell you the truth. This poor widow gave only two small coins. But she really gave more than all those rich people. The rich have plenty; they gave only what they did not need. This woman is very poor. But she gave all she had. And she needed that money to help her live.'" Mark 12:41–44

Write what you would do if you had $10.00 to give away and you could not keep it for yourself.

This Lady Gave the Smallest Offering in the World

Exclusive interview by newspaper reporter Abraham Moses of the *Jerusalem News.*

Would you pick up a penny?

____

Give this story a good ending. What do you think happened to the lady?

HOW MUCH?

YOU SHOULD GIVE WHAT GOD TELLS YOU TO GIVE.

In the Old Testament, God told the people to give a tenth of everything they had to God.

> *"Be sure to set aside a tenth of all that your fields produce each year." Deuteronomy 14:22, NIV*

A tenth is 1 out of every 10.

LOOK AT THE TEN DIMES BELOW. CIRCLE ONE OF THEM. THAT IS A TENTH.

HOW MANY DIMES WOULD YOU GIVE IF YOU HAD TWENTY DIMES? CIRCLE THE CORRECT NUMBER BELOW.

the New Testament, Jesus reminds us that our attitudes are more important than how much we give.

> *"But woe to you Pharisees! For though you are careful to tithe even the smallest part of your income, you completely forget about justice and the love of God. You should tithe, yes, but you should not leave these other things undone." Luke 11:42, TLB*

Jesus reminds us that we should give because of our love for God.

What did Jesus give for us?

What can we give to God?

What Have You Learned About Giving?

True/False

Answer the questions as best you can without help from anyone else. **You can look back in the wordbook for the answers.** Write **T** for true or **F** for false in the space provided.

_____ **1.** The Bible says that we should give an offering at our church even if it makes us sad.

_____ **2.** Jesus told about the widow who gave ten gold coins in the offering.

_____ **3.** People give money to their church to thank God for all He's done for them.

_____ **4.** God wants us to love Him and give Him our heart.

_____ **5.** Churches collect money and save all of it in the bank.

_____ **6.** Everything we have and own also belongs to God in some way.

7. Write out in your own words what it means to love the Lord with all your heart as Jesus said God wants us to do.

8. 2 Corinthians 8:9 says that the example we should follow when we give is:

- Adam and Eve
- Samson
- Jesus Christ
- Moses

9. The most important treasures we have should be stored in:

- the bank in our town
- God's bank in heaven

Now have a parent or teacher grade your quiz.

Alex and the Lemonade Stand

"So, what are you going to do with all the money?" Mr. Jones asked as he took the glass of lemonade that Alex handed him. Alex smiled as he thanked Mr. Jones for the fifty cents.

"I saw this new game at the store. If I can raise $10.00, I'll be able to buy it."

Mr. Jones drank the lemonade and handed the glass back to Alex. "Well, good luck."

"Thank you! Come again!" Alex called out as Mr. Jones continued walking down the street.

The sun was beating down on Alex, but he didn't mind. The hotter the day, the more lemonade he would sell. He looked down at his money box. It had been a great day. Almost everyone who walked by had stopped to buy a glass of lemonade. Mrs. Parker had gotten each of her twins a glass. Bobby, his next-door neighbor, had come out just to buy some lemonade.

There was only a little bit of lemonade left in the pitcher when Amy stopped by. "I'll have a glass of lemonade," she said as she handed Alex fifty cents.

"You're in luck," Alex replied. "This is the last of it." Amy quickly drank the cool drink. "Yum! This sure tastes good on a hot day." She handed the glass back and turned to go. "See you tomorrow in church."

"See you tomorrow!" Alex called as Amy rode off on her bike. Alex was excited as he counted his money. Ten dollars! It was just enough for the game he wanted to buy. Suddenly, he remembered what Amy had said. Church! He had forgotten all about it. He looked at his money box. What should he do? He really wanted that game, but if he bought it, he wouldn't have any money left to put in the offering. But if he took some of the money for the offering, he'd have to wait another week to raise the rest of the ten dollars.

Alex thought about what to do as he cleaned up his lemonade stand. He really wanted that game. But Alex loved Jesus with all his heart and wanted to please Him. He looked at the ten dollars in his hand and realized that he knew exactly what he was going to do.

IF YOU WERE ALEX, WHAT WOULD YOU DO?

WRITE HOW MUCH YOU WOULD GIVE TO GOD. ______

WRITE THE AMOUNT YOU WOULD KEEP FOR THE GAME. ______

Start Giving Now!

1. Put your offering for church in an envelope. Ask your teacher or parent to show you what your church's offering envelope looks like.

   Write the kinds of coins you put in the envelope.

   _____ Quarters= __________

   _____ Dimes= __________

   _____ Nickels= __________

   _____ Pennies= __________

2. Next, add up the total you are going to give.

   My offering totals __________

3. Put your envelope with your Bible to take to church next week.

MY OFFERING

Fill in the sample envelope below and color it or design it any way you'd like.

"He [each person] should not give if it makes him sad. God loves the person who gives happily."

2 Corinthians 9:7